DeepSeek : The Ultimate G Creating Content
By: Ra E J Wallace

Table of Contents

Disclaimer: This book was created with AI assistance. While effort has been made to ensure accuracy, the content is for informational purposes only.

Chapter 1: Introduction to DeepSeek AI

Chapter 1, Introduction to

DeepSeek AI

What is DeepSeek AI?

DeepSeek AI is an advanced artificial intelligence platform designed to assist content creators in generating, optimizing, and managing content across various formats and platforms. Leveraging cutting-edge technologies like Natural Language Processing (NLP) and machine learning, DeepSeek AI empowers creators to produce high-quality content efficiently and effectively.

The Evolution of AI in Content Creation

The integration of AI into content creation has revolutionized the way we produce and consume information. From simple spell-checkers to sophisticated content generators, AI has come a long way. DeepSeek AI represents the next step in this evolution, offering tools that not only automate mundane tasks but also enhance creativity and innovation.

Why Content Creators Need DeepSeek AI

In today's fast-paced digital landscape, content creators face immense pressure to produce engaging, relevant, and high-quality content consistently. DeepSeek AI addresses these challenges by providing tools that streamline the content creation process, improve accuracy, and unlock new creative possibilities.

Chapter 2: Understanding DeepSeek AI's Core Features

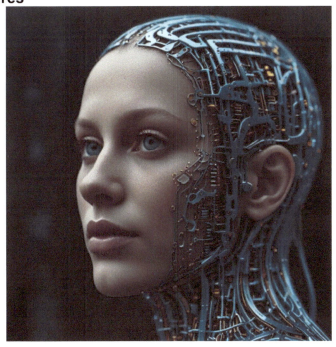

Natural Language Processing (NLP)

At the heart of DeepSeek AI is its advanced NLP capabilities, which enable the platform to understand, interpret, and generate human-like text. This technology allows DeepSeek AI to assist with tasks ranging from writing and editing to summarizing and translating content.

Content Generation and Optimization

DeepSeek AI can generate content from scratch or optimize existing content to make it more engaging and effective. Whether you need a blog post, social media update, or email campaign, DeepSeek AI can help you craft compelling messages that resonate with your audience.

SEO and Keyword Analysis

Search engine optimization (SEO) is crucial for ensuring your content reaches the right audience. DeepSeek AI's SEO tools analyze keywords, suggest improvements, and help you optimize your content for better search engine rankings.

Plagiarism Detection and Originality

Originality is key to maintaining credibility and trust with your audience. DeepSeek AI includes plagiarism detection features that ensure your content is unique and free from duplicate material.

Multilingual Support

In a globalized world, reaching a diverse audience is essential. DeepSeek AI supports multiple languages, allowing you to create and translate content for different markets and cultures.

—

Chapter 3: How DeepSeek AI Enhances Content

Creation

In the fast-paced world of content creation, efficiency, quality, and consistency are paramount. DeepSeek AI is designed to address these needs by offering tools and features that streamline workflows, enhance creativity, and elevate the overall quality of your content. Whether you're a blogger, marketer, video creator, or social media influencer, DeepSeek

AI empowers you to work smarter, not harder. Let's dive deeper into how it transforms the content creation process.

Streamlining Research and Ideation

Coming up with fresh, engaging ideas and conducting thorough research are foundational steps in content creation. However, these tasks can be time-consuming and overwhelming, especially when you're juggling multiple projects or tight deadlines. DeepSeek AI simplifies this process by acting as your intelligent research partner.

Topic Suggestions:

DeepSeek AI analyzes trending topics, audience interests, and industry trends to provide you with a steady stream of content ideas. Whether you're writing a blog post, creating a video, or planning a social media campaign, the platform ensures you never run out of inspiration.

Summarizing Research Materials:

Instead of spending hours sifting through articles, reports, and data, DeepSeek AI can summarize key points from your research materials. This allows you to quickly grasp complex information and incorporate it into your content.

- **Generating Outlines**: A well-structured outline is the backbone of any great piece of content. DeepSeek AI helps you create detailed outlines tailored to your goals, ensuring your content flows logically and effectively communicates your message.

By handling the heavy lifting of research and ideation, DeepSeek AI frees up your time to focus on the creative aspects of content creation.

Writing Assistance and Automation

Writing is at the heart of content creation, but it can also be one of the most challenging and time-consuming tasks. DeepSeek AI acts as a virtual writing assistant, providing real-time support to help you craft polished, engaging content.

Grammar and Style Suggestions:

DeepSeek AI offers real-time feedback on grammar, punctuation, and sentence structure, ensuring your writing is clear and error-free. It also provides style suggestions to help you maintain a consistent tone and voice.

Tone Adjustment:

Whether you need a professional, conversational, or persuasive tone, DeepSeek AI can adapt your writing to match your desired style. This is particularly useful when creating content for different audiences or platforms.

Automating Repetitive Tasks:

Formatting, structuring, and organizing content can be tedious. DeepSeek AI automates these tasks, allowing you to focus on the creative aspects of writing. For example, it can automatically generate headings, bullet points, and numbered lists to improve readability.

Content Expansion:

If you're struggling to flesh out an idea, DeepSeek AI can help expand your content by suggesting additional points, examples, or explanations. This ensures your content is comprehensive and engaging.

With DeepSeek AI as your writing assistant, you can produce high-quality content faster and with less effort.

—

Improving Content Quality and Consistency

Consistency is key to building a strong brand voice and establishing trust with your audience. However, maintaining consistency across multiple pieces of content can be challenging, especially when working with a team or managing multiple projects. DeepSeek AI ensures your content is not only high-quality but also aligned with your brand guidelines.

Style Analysis:

DeepSeek AI analyzes your writing style and identifies patterns in tone, vocabulary, and sentence structure. This helps you maintain a consistent voice across all your content, whether you're writing a blog post, crafting a social media caption, or drafting an email.

Brand Alignment:

The platform allows you to input your brand guidelines, such as preferred terminology, tone, and formatting rules. DeepSeek AI then ensures your content adheres to these guidelines, reinforcing your brand identity.

Quality Assurance:

DeepSeek AI goes beyond grammar and spelling checks to ensure your content is clear, concise, and impactful. It provides suggestions for improving readability, eliminating redundancies, and enhancing overall quality.

By maintaining consistency and quality, DeepSeek AI helps you build a strong, recognizable brand that resonates with your audience.

Saving Time and Boosting Productivity

Time is one of the most valuable resources for content creators. DeepSeek AI helps you maximize your productivity by automating routine tasks and providing intelligent suggestions, allowing you to focus on strategic activities and creative decision-making.

Automating Routine Tasks:

From formatting and structuring content to generating meta descriptions and alt text, DeepSeek AI handles repetitive tasks that often eat up valuable time. This allows you to focus on higher-level tasks like strategy and creativity.

Intelligent Suggestions:

DeepSeek AI provides actionable insights and suggestions to improve your content. Whether it's optimizing for SEO, enhancing readability, or refining your tone, the platform ensures your content is always at its best.

Faster Turnaround Times:

By streamlining the content creation process, DeepSeek AI enables you to produce more content in less time. This is particularly beneficial for creators who need to meet tight deadlines or manage multiple projects simultaneously.

Focus on Strategy:

With DeepSeek AI handling the technical aspects of content creation, you can dedicate more time to strategic activities like audience analysis, campaign planning, and creative brainstorming. This helps you grow your business and achieve your long-term goals.

By saving time and boosting productivity, DeepSeek AI empowers you to achieve more with less effort, giving you a competitive edge in the content creation landscape.

Universal Applications of DeepSeek AI

The benefits of DeepSeek AI extend across industries and content formats. Whether you're a solo creator, part of a team, or running a large-scale content operation, the platform's features are designed to enhance your workflow and elevate your output.

For Bloggers and Writers:

DeepSeek AI helps you generate ideas, write drafts, and optimize content for SEO, ensuring your blog posts and articles are engaging and discoverable.

For Social Media Creators:

The platform assists with crafting captions, generating hashtags, and scheduling posts, making it easier to maintain a consistent social media presence.

For Video Creators:

DeepSeek AI simplifies scriptwriting, generates subtitles, and optimizes video metadata, helping you create content that resonates with your audience.

For Marketers:

From email campaigns to ad copy, DeepSeek AI ensures your marketing content is persuasive, personalized, and optimized for conversions.

For E-commerce Brands : The platform helps you create compelling product descriptions, optimize landing pages, and engage customers with personalized content.

Conclusion

DeepSeek AI is more than just a tool—it's a transformative force in the world of content creation. By streamlining research, providing writing assistance, improving quality and consistency, and boosting productivity, the platform empowers creators to achieve their goals with greater ease and efficiency. Whether you're a seasoned professional or just starting out, DeepSeek AI is your ultimate partner in creating content that stands out and delivers results. Embrace the future of content creation and unlock your full potential with DeepSeek AI.

—

Chapter 4: DeepSeek AI for Different Types of Content

Blogging and Articles

DeepSeek AI can help you generate blog post ideas, write drafts, and optimize articles for SEO. It also provides insights into trending topics and audience preferences, ensuring your content remains relevant and engaging.

Social Media Content

Creating engaging social media content requires creativity and precision. DeepSeek AI assists with crafting captions, generating hashtags, and scheduling posts to maximize reach and engagement.

Video Scripts and Storytelling

Video content is increasingly popular, but scripting can be challenging. DeepSeek AI helps you write compelling video scripts, generate subtitles, and optimize metadata for better discoverability.

Email Marketing and Newsletters

Email marketing remains a powerful tool for connecting with your audience. DeepSeek AI helps you write persuasive email copy, personalize messages, and analyze campaign performance to improve results.

E-books and Long-Form Content

Creating long-form content like e-books requires extensive research and planning. DeepSeek AI simplifies this process by generating outlines, writing chapters, and ensuring consistency throughout the document.

Chapter 5: SEO and DeepSeek AI: A Perfect Match

Keyword Research Made Easy

DeepSeek AI's keyword research tools analyze search trends and suggest relevant keywords to target in your content. This helps you create content that aligns with what your audience is searching for.

Optimizing Content for Search Engines

DeepSeek AI provides actionable insights to optimize your content for search engines. From meta descriptions to internal linking, the platform ensures your content is fully optimized for maximum visibility.

Analyzing Competitor Content

Understanding what your competitors are doing can give you a competitive edge. DeepSeek AI analyzes competitor content to identify gaps and opportunities, helping you stay ahead in your niche.

Tracking Performance and Analytics

DeepSeek AI integrates with analytics tools to track the performance of your content. You can monitor metrics like traffic, engagement, and conversions to measure the effectiveness of your SEO efforts.

Chapter 6: DeepSeek AI for Social Media Creators

Crafting Engaging Captions and Posts

Social media success hinges on creating content that resonates with your audience. DeepSeek AI helps you craft engaging captions, generate post ideas, and tailor your content to different platforms.

Hashtag Suggestions and Trends

Hashtags are essential for increasing the reach of your social media posts. DeepSeek AI suggests relevant hashtags and identifies trending topics to help you stay relevant and visible.

Scheduling and Automation

Consistency is key to social media success. DeepSeek AI allows you to schedule posts in advance and automate your social media strategy, ensuring you maintain a consistent presence.

Analyzing Audience Engagement

Understanding how your audience interacts with your content is crucial for refining your strategy. DeepSeek AI provides insights into engagement metrics, helping you identify what works and what doesn't.

Chapter 7: DeepSeek AI for Video Content Creators

Scriptwriting and Storyboarding

Creating compelling video content starts with a strong script. DeepSeek AI assists with scriptwriting, storyboarding, and generating ideas for your videos.

Caption and Subtitle Generation

Captions and subtitles make your videos accessible to a wider audience. DeepSeek AI automatically generates accurate captions and subtitles, saving you time and effort.

Video SEO and Metadata Optimization

Optimizing your video content for search engines is essential for discoverability. DeepSeek AI helps you optimize titles, descriptions, and tags to improve your video's ranking on platforms like YouTube.

Enhancing Creativity with AI Insights

DeepSeek AI provides insights into audience preferences and trending topics, helping you create video content that resonates with your viewers and stands out from the competition.

Chapter 8: DeepSeek AI for Email Marketing

Writing Persuasive Email Copy

Email marketing success depends on crafting compelling messages that drive action. DeepSeek AI helps you write persuasive email copy that resonates with your audience and encourages engagement.

Personalization and Audience Segmentation

Personalized emails are more effective at driving conversions. DeepSeek AI helps you segment your audience and tailor your messages to individual preferences and behaviors.

A/B Testing and Optimization

A/B testing is essential for optimizing your email campaigns. DeepSeek AI assists with creating and testing different versions of your emails to identify the most effective approach.

Improving Open and Click-Through Rates

DeepSeek AI provides insights into email performance, helping you improve open and click-through rates. By analyzing metrics like subject line effectiveness and call-to-action placement, you can refine your strategy for better results.

Chapter 9: DeepSeek AI for E-commerce Content

Product Descriptions and Reviews

Compelling product descriptions and reviews are essential for driving sales. DeepSeek AI helps you create detailed, persuasive content that highlights the benefits of your products and builds trust with customers.

Ad Copy and Landing Pages

Effective ad copy and landing pages are crucial for converting visitors into customers. DeepSeek AI assists with crafting persuasive ad copy and optimizing landing pages for maximum impact.

Customer Engagement and Retention

Engaging with customers and building loyalty is key to long-term success. DeepSeek AI helps you create personalized content that fosters customer relationships and encourages repeat business.

Leveraging AI for Sales Growth

DeepSeek AI provides insights into customer behavior and preferences, helping you identify opportunities for upselling and cross-selling. By leveraging these insights, you can drive sales growth and increase revenue.

Chapter 10: DeepSeek AI for Multilingual Content Creation

Breaking Language Barriers

Reaching a global audience requires content in multiple languages. DeepSeek AI's multilingual support allows you to create and translate content for different markets, breaking down language barriers and expanding your reach.

Localization and Cultural Adaptation

Localization goes beyond translation—it involves adapting content to fit cultural nuances and preferences. DeepSeek AI helps you localize your content to resonate with diverse audiences.

Expanding Global Reach

By creating content in multiple languages, you can tap into new markets and grow your audience. DeepSeek AI's multilingual capabilities make it easier to expand your global presence.

Ensuring Accuracy and Fluency

Accuracy and fluency are essential for effective multilingual content. DeepSeek AI ensures your translations are accurate and natural-sounding, maintaining the quality and integrity of your content.

Chapter 11: Ethical Considerations in AI-Generated Content

Maintaining Authenticity and Transparency

While AI can enhance content creation, it's important to maintain authenticity and transparency. DeepSeek AI encourages creators to disclose the use of AI tools and ensure their content reflects their unique voice and perspective.

Avoiding Plagiarism and Copyright Issues

Originality is crucial for maintaining credibility. DeepSeek AI's plagiarism detection features help you avoid unintentional plagiarism and ensure your content is original and compliant with copyright laws.

Balancing AI and Human Creativity

AI is a powerful tool, but it should complement, not replace, human creativity. DeepSeek AI encourages creators to use AI as a collaborative partner, enhancing their creative process rather than relying on it entirely.

Ethical Use of AI in Content Creation

As AI becomes more prevalent, it's important to use it ethically. DeepSeek AI promotes responsible use of AI tools, ensuring they are used to enhance content creation without compromising ethical standards.

Chapter 12: Integrating DeepSeek AI into Your

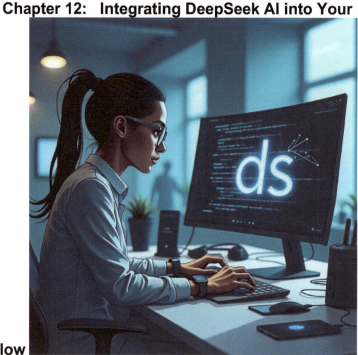

Workflow

Integrating DeepSeek AI into your content creation workflow is a game-changer, but it requires a thoughtful approach to ensure seamless adoption and maximum efficiency. This chapter provides a comprehensive guide to setting up, customizing, and collaborating with DeepSeek AI, along with best practices to help you get the most out of the platform. Whether you're a solo creator or part of a team, these insights will help you harness the full potential of AI in your creative process.

Setting Up and Getting Started

Integrating DeepSeek AI into your workflow is designed to be intuitive and user-friendly. Here's a step-by-step guide to help you get started:

1. Create an Account:

Begin by signing up for DeepSeek AI on their official website. Choose a subscription plan that aligns with your needs, whether you're an individual creator or part of a larger team .

2. Onboarding Process:

DeepSeek AI offers an onboarding tutorial to familiarize you with its features. Take advantage of this to understand the platform's capabilities and interface .

3. Install Integrations:

DeepSeek AI integrates with popular tools like Google Docs, WordPress, and social media platforms. Install these integrations to streamline your workflow and ensure seamless content transfer.

4. Set Up Your Profile:

Customize your profile by inputting your brand guidelines, preferred tone, and style preferences. This ensures the AI generates content that aligns with your unique voice.

5. Test the Platform:

Start with a small project, such as drafting a blog post or generating social media captions, to get a feel for how DeepSeek AI works. Experiment with different features to see how they can enhance your workflow.

By following these steps, you'll be well on your way to integrating DeepSeek AI into your daily routine.

Customizing AI Tools for Your Needs

DeepSeek AI is highly customizable, allowing you to tailor the platform to your specific requirements. Here's how to make the most of its customization options:

1. Configure Settings:

Adjust the platform's settings to match your workflow. For example, you can set default tones (e.g., professional, casual, persuasive) or enable specific features like SEO optimization or plagiarism detection.

2. Create Templates:

Save time by creating templates for recurring content types, such as blog posts, email newsletters, or social media updates. DeepSeek AI can use these templates to generate content quickly and consistently.

3. **Optimize for Your Workflow:** Customize the platform's interface to prioritize the tools you use most often. For instance, if you frequently use SEO analysis, make sure it's easily accessible from your dashboard.

4. Set Up Collaboration Features:

If you're working with a team, configure DeepSeek AI's collaboration tools to allow multiple users to access and edit content. This ensures everyone stays on the same page and maintains consistency.

5. **Integrate with Other Tools:** DeepSeek AI works seamlessly with tools like Grammarly, Trello, and Slack. Set up these integrations to create a unified workflow that maximizes efficiency.

By customizing DeepSeek AI to fit your needs, you can create a personalized content creation ecosystem that works for you.

Collaborating with AI as a Creative Partner

AI is not just a tool—it's a creative partner that can enhance your work and inspire new ideas. Here's how to collaborate effectively with DeepSeek AI:

1. Leverage Real-Time Suggestions:

Use DeepSeek AI's real-time feedback to refine your writing as you go. Whether it's improving grammar, adjusting tone, or enhancing readability, the platform provides actionable insights to elevate your content.

2. Generate Ideas Together:

Stuck in a creative rut? Use DeepSeek AI's brainstorming tools to generate fresh ideas. The platform can suggest topics, angles, and even headlines to spark your creativity.

3. Iterate and Improve:

Treat DeepSeek AI as a sounding board for your ideas. Use its suggestions to iterate on your content, experimenting with different approaches until you find the perfect fit.

4. Combine AI and Human Creativity: While AI can handle repetitive tasks and provide suggestions, your unique perspective and creativity are irreplaceable. Use DeepSeek AI to enhance your work, not replace it.

5. Learn from AI Insights:

DeepSeek AI provides analytics and performance metrics for your content. Use these insights to identify trends, understand what resonates with your audience, and refine your strategy.

By collaborating with DeepSeek AI, you can unlock new levels of creativity and efficiency in your content creation process.

Best Practices for Seamless Integration

To get the most out of DeepSeek AI, it's important to follow best practices for integration. Here are some tips and strategies to ensure a smooth and effective workflow:

1. **Start Small:**

 Begin by integrating DeepSeek AI into one aspect of your workflow, such as blog writing or social media content creation. Once you're comfortable, gradually expand its use to other areas.

2. **Train Your Team:**

If you're working with a team, provide training sessions to ensure everyone understands how to use DeepSeek AI effectively. This will help maintain consistency and maximize productivity.

3. **Set Clear Goals:**

Define what you want to achieve with DeepSeek AI, whether it's saving time, improving content quality, or boosting SEO performance. Having clear goals will help you measure success and optimize your use of the platform.

4. **Monitor Performance:**

Regularly review the performance of your content created with DeepSeek AI. Use analytics tools to track metrics like engagement, traffic, and conversions, and adjust your strategy as needed.

5. Stay Updated:

 DeepSeek AI is constantly evolving, with new features and updates being released regularly. Stay informed about these changes to ensure you're always using the platform to its full potential.

6. Maintain a Human Touch:

While AI can handle many tasks, it's important to maintain a human touch in your content. Review and edit AI-generated content to ensure it aligns with your brand voice and resonates with your audience.

7. Experiment and Innovate:

Don't be afraid to experiment with DeepSeek AI's features. Try new tools, test different approaches, and explore creative possibilities to discover what works best for you.

By following these best practices, you can seamlessly integrate DeepSeek AI into your workflow and achieve your content creation goals with greater ease and efficiency.

Solutions to Common Challenges

Integrating AI into your workflow can come with challenges. Here are some solutions to common issues:

1. **Challenge: Over-Reliance on AI**

   Solution: Use DeepSeek AI as a supplement to your creativity, not a replacement. Always review and refine AI-generated content to ensure it aligns with your vision and brand.

2. **Challenge: Learning Curve**

   Solution: Take advantage of DeepSeek AI's onboarding resources, tutorials, and customer support to quickly get up to speed. Start with simple tasks and gradually explore advanced features.

3. **Challenge: Maintaining Consistency**

   Solution: Use DeepSeek AI's style analysis and brand alignment tools to ensure all content adheres to your guidelines. Regularly update your profile with any changes to your brand voice or tone.

4. **Challenge: Integration with Existing Tools**

   Solution: DeepSeek AI offers integrations with popular tools like WordPress, Google Docs, and Slack. Set up these integrations to create a seamless workflow that minimizes disruptions.

5. **Challenge: Measuring ROI**

Solution: Track key performance metrics, such as content engagement, traffic, and conversions, to measure the impact of DeepSeek AI on your content creation process. Use these insights to refine your strategy and maximize ROI.

Conclusion

Integrating DeepSeek AI into your workflow is a transformative step that can enhance your creativity, efficiency, and productivity. By setting up the platform thoughtfully, customizing it to your needs, collaborating effectively, and following best practices, you can unlock the full potential of AI in your content creation process. Whether you're a blogger, marketer, video creator, or social media influencer, DeepSeek AI is your ultimate partner in creating content that stands out and delivers results. Embrace the future of content creation and take your work to the next level with DeepSeek AI..

Chapter 13: Case Studies: Success Stories with DeepSeek AI

DeepSeek AI has become an indispensable tool for content creators across industries, helping them streamline workflows, enhance creativity, and achieve measurable success. This chapter dives into real-world case studies, showcasing how bloggers, social media influencers, video creators, and e-commerce brands have leveraged DeepSeek AI to transform their content creation processes. These success stories highlight the platform's versatility and its ability to deliver tangible results.

Bloggers and Writers

Bloggers and writers face the constant challenge of producing high-quality content consistently while managing tight deadlines. DeepSeek AI has emerged as a game-changer for many in this space, enabling them to streamline their workflows and focus on storytelling.

Case Study 1: The Travel Blogger

Challenge: A travel blogger struggled to keep up with the demand for fresh content while juggling research, writing, and editing.

Solution : The blogger integrated DeepSeek AI into their workflow to automate research and generate outlines for blog posts.

Results:

Time Savings: Reduced research time by 50%, allowing the blogger to focus on writing and exploring new destinations.

Improved Quality: DeepSeek AI's grammar and style suggestions helped polish posts, resulting in a 30% increase in reader engagement.

SEO Boost: The platform's SEO tools optimized blog posts for search engines, leading to a 40% increase in organic traffic.

Case Study 2: The Freelance Writer

Challenge: A freelance writer needed to produce multiple articles per week for different clients, each with unique tone and style requirements.

Solution: DeepSeek AI's customization features allowed the writer to create templates for each client, ensuring consistency and efficiency.

Results:

Increased Output: The writer doubled their weekly output without compromising quality.

Client Satisfaction: Clients praised the consistency and professionalism of the content, leading to repeat business and referrals.

Creative Freedom: With AI handling repetitive tasks, the writer had more time to focus on crafting compelling narratives.

Social Media Influencers

Social media influencers thrive on engagement, but creating fresh, relatable content daily can be exhausting. DeepSeek AI has empowered influencers to stay ahead of trends and maintain a strong connection with their audience.

Case Study 3: The Lifestyle Influencer

Challenge: A lifestyle influencer struggled to come up with engaging captions and hashtags for their Instagram posts.

Solution: DeepSeek AI's caption generator and hashtag suggestions provided creative ideas tailored to the influencer's niche.

Results:

Higher Engagement: Post engagement increased by 25%, with followers praising the relatable and witty captions.

Time Saving : The influencer saved 10+ hours per week, allowing them to focus on creating visually stunning content.

Trend Awareness : DeepSeek AI's trend analysis helped the influencer stay ahead of viral topics, boosting their relevance.

Case Study 4: The Fitness Influencer

Challenge : A fitness influencer needed to create consistent content across multiple platforms, including Instagram, TikTok, and YouTube.

Solution : DeepSeek AI's cross-platform content generator helped the influencer repurpose content efficiently.

Results:

Consistent Posting : The influencer maintained a consistent posting schedule across all platforms, growing their combined follower count by 35%.

Audience Growth : DeepSeek AI's hashtag and trend suggestions helped the influencer reach new audiences, resulting in a 50% increase in TikTok followers.

Time Efficiency : The influencer saved 15+ hours per week, enabling them to focus on creating workout videos and engaging with their community.

Video Creators and YouTubers

Video content is booming, but scripting, editing, and optimizing videos can be time-consuming. DeepSeek AI has become a trusted ally for video creators, helping them streamline their processes and enhance their content.

Case Study 5: The Tech Reviewer

Challenge : A tech YouTuber spent hours scripting and editing videos, leaving little time for research and audience engagement.

Solution : DeepSeek AI's scriptwriting and subtitle generation tools automated these tasks, freeing up the creator's time .

Results :

Faster Production : Video production time decreased by 40%, allowing the creator to upload more frequently.

Improved Accessibility : Auto-generated subtitles made videos accessible to a global audience, increasing views by 20%.

Enhanced Quality : DeepSeek AI's script suggestions improved the flow and clarity of videos, leading to higher viewer retention.

Case Study 6: The Storyteller

Challenge : A documentary filmmaker needed help organizing research and drafting scripts for complex narratives.

Solution : DeepSeek AI's research summarization and outline generation tools streamlined the pre-production process.

Results :

Efficient Research : The filmmaker saved 30+ hours per project, enabling them to focus on storytelling and cinematography.

Stronger Scripts : AI-generated outlines provided a solid foundation for scripts, resulting in more cohesive and impactful stories.

Award Recognition : One of the filmmaker's documentaries, created with DeepSeek AI's assistance, won a regional film festival award.

E-commerce Brands and Marketers

E-commerce brands rely on compelling product descriptions, ad copy, and marketing campaigns to drive sales. DeepSeek AI has proven to be a valuable asset for marketers looking to optimize their content and boost conversions.

Case Study 7: The Fashion Brand**

Challenge : A fashion brand struggled to create unique product descriptions for hundreds of items in their catalog.

Solution : DeepSeek AI's product description generator produced engaging, SEO-friendly copy for each item.

Results :

Increased Sales : Conversion rates improved by 15%, with customers praising the detailed and persuasive descriptions.

Time Savings : The brand saved 20+ hours per week, allowing their team to focus on other marketing initiatives.

SEO Benefits : Optimized descriptions led to a 25% increase in organic search traffic.

Case Study 8: The Digital Marketer

Challenge : A digital marketer needed to create high-performing ad copy for multiple campaigns across platforms like Facebook, Google, and Instagram.

Solution : DeepSeek AI's ad copy generator provided tailored suggestions for each platform, ensuring consistency and effectiveness.

Results :

Higher CTR : Click-through rates increased by 30%, with ads resonating better with target audiences.

Cost Efficiency : The marketer reduced ad spend by 20% while maintaining the same level of performance.

Scalability : DeepSeek AI enabled the marketer to manage multiple campaigns simultaneously, increasing overall productivity.

Key Takeaways from Success Stories

These case studies demonstrate the transformative impact of DeepSeek AI across various industries and content formats. Here are the key takeaways:

1. **Time Efficiency :** DeepSeek AI significantly reduces the time spent on repetitive tasks, allowing creators to focus on strategy and creativity.

2. **Improved Quality :** AI-generated suggestions and optimizations enhance the quality of content, leading to higher engagement and better results.

3. **Scalability :** Whether you're a solo creator or part of a team, DeepSeek AI enables you to scale your content production without compromising quality.

4. **Audience Growth :** By leveraging AI for SEO, trend analysis, and personalization, creators can reach new audiences and grow their following.

5. **Versatility :** DeepSeek AI's tools are adaptable to various content formats, from blogs and social media posts to videos and e-commerce listings.

Conclusion

The success stories of bloggers, influencers, video creators, and e-commerce brands highlight the transformative power of DeepSeek AI. By automating repetitive tasks, enhancing creativity, and optimizing content for performance, the platform empowers creators to achieve their goals and stay ahead in a competitive landscape. Whether you're looking to save time, improve quality, or grow your audience, DeepSeek AI is your ultimate partner in content creation. Embrace the future of AI and unlock your full potential as a creator.

Chapter 14: Future Trends in AI and Content

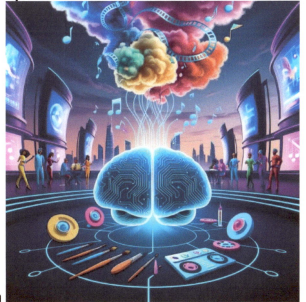

Creation

The world of content creation is undergoing a seismic shift, driven by rapid advancements in artificial

intelligence. As AI technologies continue to evolve, they are reshaping how content is created, distributed, and consumed. This chapter delves into the future of AI in content creation, exploring emerging technologies, the evolution of DeepSeek AI, and how creators can prepare for the next wave of innovation. By understanding these trends, you can stay ahead of the curve and leverage AI to its fullest potential.

The Role of AI in the Future of Content

AI is no longer a futuristic concept—it's a present-day reality that is transforming the content creation landscape. Here's how AI will shape the future of the industry:

1. **Personalization at Scale :** AI enables hyper-personalized content tailored to individual preferences, behaviors, and demographics. In the future, content creators will use AI to deliver highly targeted messages that resonate with specific audience segments, driving engagement and loyalty.

2. **Automation of Repetitive Tasks :** From drafting blog posts to scheduling social media updates, AI will continue to automate routine tasks, freeing up creators to focus on strategy and creativity.

3. **Enhanced Creativity :** AI tools like DeepSeek AI will act as creative collaborators, offering suggestions, generating ideas, and even co-creating content. This will empower creators to push boundaries and explore new formats.

4. **Real-Time Content Optimization :** AI will enable real-time optimization of content based on audience feedback and performance metrics. For example, AI can adjust headlines, visuals, or calls-to-action to maximize engagement.

5. **Multilingual and Multicultural Content :** As global audiences grow, AI will play a crucial role in creating and translating content for diverse markets, ensuring cultural relevance and linguistic accuracy.

6. **Ethical and Responsible AI Use :** As AI becomes more pervasive, ethical considerations will take center stage. Content creators will need to balance automation with authenticity, ensuring transparency and accountability in their use of AI.

By embracing these trends, content creators can position themselves at the forefront of the industry, delivering innovative and impactful content.

Emerging Technologies and Innovations

The future of AI in content creation is fueled by groundbreaking technologies. Here are some of the most exciting innovations on the horizon:

1. Generative AI : Tools like GPT-4 and beyond are revolutionizing content creation by generating text, images, and even videos. These technologies will enable creators to produce high-quality content faster and more efficiently.

2. Advanced Natural Language Processing (NLP) : NLP is becoming more sophisticated, allowing AI to understand context, tone, and nuance. This will improve the quality of AI-generated content and make it indistinguishable from human-created work.

3. AI-Powered Visual Content : AI is expanding beyond text to create visual content, such as infographics, animations, and even deep fake videos. Tools like DALL·E and MidJourney are already pushing the boundaries of what's possible.

4. Voice and Audio AI : Voice assistants and AI-generated audio content are becoming increasingly popular. In the future, creators will use AI to produce podcasts, voiceovers, and even music tailored to specific audiences.

5. Predictive Analytics : AI will use predictive analytics to forecast content trends, audience preferences, and performance outcomes. This will help creators stay ahead of the curve and produce content that resonates.

6. Immersive Technologies : AI will play a key role in creating immersive content, such as virtual reality (VR) and augmented reality (AR) experiences. These technologies will open up new possibilities for storytelling and audience engagement.

7. Blockchain and AI Integration : Blockchain technology can enhance AI by ensuring transparency and security in content creation. For example, blockchain can be used to verify the authenticity of AI-generated content or track its distribution.

These emerging technologies will redefine the content creation process, offering creators new tools and opportunities to innovate.

How DeepSeek AI is Evolving

DeepSeek AI is at the forefront of AI-driven content creation, continuously evolving to meet the needs of creators. Here's a look at the platform's development roadmap and future features:

1. Enhanced Multilingual Capabilities : DeepSeek AI is expanding its support for additional languages and dialects, enabling creators to reach global audiences with ease.

2. AI-Powered Visual Content Creation : Future updates will include tools for generating and optimizing visual content, such as infographics, social media images, and video thumbnails.

3. Real-Time Collaboration : DeepSeek AI is developing features that allow teams to collaborate in real-time, with AI providing instant feedback and suggestions.

4. Advanced SEO and Analytics : The platform will introduce more sophisticated SEO tools, including predictive keyword analysis and competitor benchmarking, to help creators optimize their content for search engines.

5. Ethical AI Features : DeepSeek AI is committed to ethical AI use. Future updates will include features that promote transparency, such as watermarking AI-generated content and providing usage guidelines.

6. Integration with Emerging Technologies : DeepSeek AI plans to integrate with immersive technologies like VR and AR, enabling creators to produce cutting-edge content.

7. Personalized Learning and Training: The platform will offer personalized training modules to help creators master AI tools and stay updated on the latest trends.

By staying ahead of industry trends and continuously innovating, DeepSeek AI ensures that creators have access to the most advanced tools and features.

Preparing for the Next Wave of AI Tools

As AI technology advances, content creators must adapt to stay competitive. Here are some tips for preparing for the next wave of AI tools:

1. **Stay Informed :** Keep up with the latest developments in AI and content creation by following industry blogs, attending webinars, and participating in online communities.

2. **Experiment with New Tools :** Don't be afraid to try out new AI tools and features. Experimentation will help you discover what works best for your workflow and creative process.

3. **Invest in Training :** Take advantage of training resources, such as tutorials, courses, and certifications, to build your skills and stay ahead of the curve.

4. **Focus on Creativity :** While AI can handle many tasks, your creativity and unique perspective are irreplaceable. Use AI as a tool to enhance your work, not replace it.

5. **Embrace Collaboration :** AI is most effective when used in collaboration with human creativity. Treat AI as a creative partner and leverage its strengths to complement your own.

6. **Prioritize Ethical Use :** As AI becomes more pervasive, ethical considerations will become increasingly important. Ensure your use of AI is transparent, responsible, and aligned with your values.

7. Adapt to Audience Needs : Use AI to gain insights into your audience's preferences and behaviors. Tailor your content to meet their needs and stay relevant in a rapidly changing landscape.

By preparing for the next wave of AI tools, you can position yourself as a leader in the content creation industry and continue to deliver innovative, impactful work.

Solutions to Future Challenges

As AI continues to evolve, content creators will face new challenges. Here are some solutions to common issues:

1. Challenge: Keeping Up with Rapid Changes

Solution : Dedicate time to continuous learning and experimentation. Stay connected with industry trends and be open to adopting new tools and technologies.

2. Challenge: Balancing Automation and Authenticity

Solution : Use AI to handle repetitive tasks and enhance your work, but always review and refine AI-generated content to ensure it aligns with your brand voice and values.

3. Challenge: Ethical Concerns

Solution : Follow best practices for ethical AI use, such as disclosing AI-generated content, avoiding plagiarism, and ensuring transparency in your creative process.

4. Challenge : Competition from AI-Generated Content**

Solution : Focus on creating unique, high-quality content that showcases your creativity and expertise. Use AI to enhance your work, not replace it.

5. Challenge: Adapting to New Formats

Solution : Experiment with emerging formats, such as VR, AR, and interactive content, to stay ahead of the curve and engage your audience in new ways.

Conclusion

The future of AI in content creation is bright, offering endless possibilities for innovation and growth. By understanding emerging trends, leveraging evolving tools like DeepSeek AI, and preparing for the next wave of AI advancements, content creators can stay ahead of the curve and continue to deliver impactful, engaging content. Embrace the future of AI and unlock your full potential as a creator in this exciting new era.

—

Chapter 15: Tips and Tricks for Maximizing DeepSeek AI

DeepSeek AI is a versatile and powerful tool, but unlocking its full potential requires a deeper understanding of its features and capabilities. This chapter provides actionable tips and tricks to help you maximize the platform's potential, combine AI with human

creativity, stay ahead of the competition, and embrace continuous learning. Whether you're a beginner or an advanced user, these insights will help you elevate your content creation game.

Advanced Features and Hidden Gems

DeepSeek AI is packed with advanced features and hidden gems that can take your content creation to the next level. Here's how to make the most of them:

1. Customizable Tone and Style :

How to Use : DeepSeek AI allows you to customize the tone and style of your content to match your brand voice. Use the "Tone Settings" feature to select options like professional, casual, or persuasive.

Pro Tip : Save multiple tone profiles for different types of content (e.g., one for blog posts, another for social media captions).

2. SEO Optimization Tools :

How to Use : DeepSeek AI's SEO tools analyze your content and suggest improvements for better search engine rankings. Use the "SEO Analyzer" to identify high-ranking keywords and optimize meta descriptions.

Pro Tip : Combine SEO suggestions with your own keyword research for even better results.

3. Plagiarism Detection :

How to Use : Ensure your content is original by running it through DeepSeek AI's plagiarism checker. The tool highlights duplicate content and suggests revisions.

Pro Tip : Use this feature before publishing to maintain credibility and avoid penalties from search engines.

4. Multilingual Content Creation :

How to Use : DeepSeek AI supports multiple languages, making it easy to create and translate content for global audiences. Use the "Language Settings" to switch between languages.

Pro Tip : Localize your content by adapting it to cultural nuances and regional preferences.

5. Content Templates :

How to Use : Save time by using DeepSeek AI's pre-built templates for blogs, social media posts, emails, and more. Customize these templates to suit your needs.

Pro Tip : Create your own templates for recurring content types to streamline your workflow.

6. Real-Time Collaboration :

How to Use : If you're working with a team, use DeepSeek AI's collaboration tools to share projects, provide feedback, and co-create content in real time.

Pro Tip : Assign roles and permissions to team members to ensure smooth collaboration.

7. Analytics and Performance Tracking :

How to Use : DeepSeek AI provides insights into how your content is performing. Use the "Analytics Dashboard" to track metrics like engagement, traffic, and conversions.

Pro Tip : Use these insights to refine your content strategy and focus on what works best.

Combining AI with Human Creativity

While AI is a powerful tool, human creativity is irreplaceable. Here's how to strike the perfect balance:

1. Use AI as a Starting Point :

- **Let DeepSeek AI generate ideas, outlines, or drafts, but add your unique perspective to make the content truly yours.**

- **Example:** Use AI to brainstorm blog topics, but craft the final post with your personal insights and experiences.

2. Edit and Refine AI-Generated Content :

- **AI can produce high-quality content, but it's up to you to polish it. Review and edit AI-generated text to ensure it aligns with your voice and goals.**

- **Example:** Adjust the tone, add anecdotes, or rephrase sentences to make the content more engaging.

3. **Experiment with Creative Formats :**

   - Use DeepSeek AI to explore new content formats, such as interactive posts, quizzes, or infographics. Combine these formats with your creative vision to stand out.

   - Example: Use AI to generate data points for an infographic, then design it using your favorite graphic tools.

4. **Collaborate with AI as a Partner :**

   - Treat DeepSeek AI as a creative partner rather than just a tool. Use its suggestions to spark new ideas and push the boundaries of your creativity.

   - Example: If you're stuck on a script, use AI to generate alternative scenes or dialogue options.

5. **Maintain Authenticity :**

   - While AI can handle many tasks, your authenticity is what resonates with your audience. Ensure your content reflects your values, personality, and brand identity.

   - Example: Add personal stories or behind-the-scenes insights to AI-generated content to make it more relatable.

Staying Ahead of the Competition

In a competitive landscape, staying ahead requires innovation and strategy. Here's how to leverage DeepSeek AI to outpace your competitors:

1. **Leverage Predictive Analytics :**

- **Use DeepSeek AI's analytics tools to identify emerging trends and audience preferences. Create content that aligns with these insights to stay relevant.**

- **Example:** If analytics show a growing interest in sustainability, create content around eco-friendly practices.

2. **Optimize for SEO :**

- **Use DeepSeek AI's SEO tools to ensure your content ranks higher than your competitors'. Focus on long-tail keywords and optimize for voice search.**

- **Example:** Target niche keywords like "best budget travel tips for students" to attract a specific audience.

3. **Create Evergreen Content :**

- **Use DeepSeek AI to generate timeless content that remains relevant long after publication. This helps you maintain a steady stream of traffic.**

- **Example:** Write "how-to" guides or listicles that address common pain points in your niche.

4. **Experiment with New Formats :**

- **Stay ahead by experimenting with emerging content formats, such as short-form videos, podcasts, or interactive posts. Use DeepSeek AI to generate ideas and scripts.**

- **Example:** Use AI to create a script for a TikTok series that explains complex topics in simple terms.

5. Monitor Competitor Strategies :

- **Use DeepSeek AI to analyze your competitors' content and identify gaps or opportunities. Adapt your strategy to fill these gaps and differentiate yourself.**

- **Example:** If competitors are focusing on written content, create video content to stand out.

Continuous Learning and Adaptation

The world of AI is constantly evolving, and staying relevant requires continuous learning and adaptation. Here's how to keep up:

1. **Stay Updated on AI Trends :**

- **Follow AI blogs, attend webinars, and participate in online communities to stay informed about the latest developments.**

- **Example:** Subscribe to newsletters like "AI Weekly" or join forums like Reddit's r/MachineLearning.

2. **Explore New Features :**

- **DeepSeek AI regularly updates its platform with new features. Take the time to explore these updates and incorporate them into your workflow.**

- **Example:** If DeepSeek AI introduces a new visual content tool, experiment with it to enhance your social media posts.

3. **Invest in Training :**

- **Take advantage of DeepSeek AI's tutorials, courses, and certifications to build your skills and stay ahead of the curve.**

- **Example:** Complete a course on "Advanced SEO Strategies with DeepSeek AI" to optimize your content further.

4. **Experiment and Innovate :**

- **Don't be afraid to experiment with new tools, formats, and strategies. Use DeepSeek AI to test different approaches and learn from the results.**

- **Example:** Try using AI to create a podcast script or an interactive quiz for your audience.

5. **Seek Feedback :**

- **Regularly seek feedback from your audience and peers to understand what's working and what's not. Use this feedback to refine your content strategy.**

- **Example:** Conduct surveys or polls to gauge audience preferences and adjust your content accordingly.

Conclusion

DeepSeek AI is a powerful ally in your content creation journey, but its true potential lies in how you use it. By exploring advanced features, combining AI with human creativity, staying ahead of the competition, and embracing continuous learning, you can unlock new levels of success.

Whether you're a blogger, marketer, video creator, or e-commerce brand, DeepSeek AI provides the tools and insights you need to thrive in a competitive landscape. Embrace the future of content creation and let DeepSeek AI be your guide to innovation and excellence.

Chapter 16: FAQs About DeepSeek AI for Content Creators

DeepSeek AI is a powerful tool designed to revolutionize content creation, but like any new technology, it can raise questions and concerns. This chapter addresses the most frequently asked questions about DeepSeek AI, offering solutions, troubleshooting tips, and insights into pricing and comparisons with other tools. Whether you're a beginner or an experienced user, this guide will help you navigate the platform with confidence.

Common Questions and Concerns

Here are answers to some of the most common questions and concerns about DeepSeek AI:

1. What is DeepSeek AI, and how does it work?

DeepSeek AI is an artificial intelligence platform that assists content creators with tasks like writing, editing, SEO optimization, and idea generation. It uses advanced Natural Language Processing (NLP) and machine learning to understand context, generate text, and provide actionable insights.

2. Is DeepSeek AI suitable for beginners?

Yes! DeepSeek AI is designed to be user-friendly, with an intuitive interface and onboarding tutorials to help beginners get started quickly. Even if you're new to AI tools, you'll find it easy to integrate into your workflow.

3. Can DeepSeek AI replace human writers?

No. DeepSeek AI is a tool to enhance creativity and productivity, not replace human writers. It handles repetitive tasks and provides suggestions, but your unique perspective and creativity are essential for producing authentic, engaging content.

4. How does DeepSeek AI ensure content originality?

DeepSeek AI includes built-in plagiarism detection tools to ensure your content is original. It also provides suggestions to improve uniqueness and avoid unintentional duplication.

5. Is DeepSeek AI compatible with other tools?

Yes. DeepSeek AI integrates seamlessly with popular platforms like Google Docs, WordPress, and social media schedulers. This ensures a smooth workflow across different tools.

6. Can DeepSeek AI create content in multiple languages?

Absolutely. DeepSeek AI supports multiple languages, making it ideal for creators targeting global audiences. It also ensures translations are accurate and culturally relevant.

7. How secure is my data with DeepSeek AI?

DeepSeek AI prioritizes data security and privacy. Your content and personal information are encrypted and stored securely, with strict access controls in place.

Troubleshooting and Support

Encountering issues? Here are some troubleshooting tips and support options to help you resolve challenges:

1. Issue: AI-generated content doesn't match my tone or style.

Solution : Customize your profile settings to reflect your preferred tone, style, and brand guidelines. DeepSeek AI will adapt its suggestions to align with your unique voice.

2. Issue: The platform is slow or unresponsive.

Solution : Check your internet connection and ensure your browser is up to date. If the issue persists, clear your cache or try accessing the platform from a different device.

3. Issue: I'm not getting the desired SEO results.

Solution : Double-check your keyword inputs and ensure you're using DeepSeek AI's SEO optimization tools effectively. You can also consult the platform's tutorials or reach out to support for guidance.

4. Issue: I'm struggling to integrate DeepSeek AI with other tools.

Solution : Visit the integrations section in your account settings for step-by-step instructions. If you're still having trouble, contact DeepSeek AI's support team for assistance.

5. Issue: I'm unsure how to use a specific feature.

Solution : Explore DeepSeek AI's knowledge base, which includes tutorials, FAQs, and video guides. You can also join the platform's community forum to ask questions and share tips with other users.

6. How to Access Support :

Live Chat : Available on the DeepSeek AI website for instant assistance.

Email Support : Send your queries to support@deepseekai.com.

Help Center : Access tutorials, guides, and troubleshooting articles in the Help Center.

Pricing and Subscription Plans

DeepSeek AI offers flexible pricing plans to suit different needs and budgets. Here's an overview of the available options:

1. **Free Plan**

Features : Basic writing assistance, limited access to SEO tools, and a set number of content generations per month.

Best For : Beginners or creators who want to test the platform before committing.

2. **Pro Plan**

Price : $29/month (billed annually) or $39/month (billed monthly).

Features : Advanced writing and editing tools, full access to SEO optimization, plagiarism detection, and multilingual support.

Best For : Individual creators and freelancers who need robust tools for consistent content creation.

3. **Team Plan**

Price : $99/month (billed annually) or $129/month (billed monthly).

Features : All Pro features, plus collaboration tools, team management, and priority support.

Best For : Small teams and agencies working on multiple projects.

4. Enterprise Plan

Price : Custom pricing based on requirements.

Features : All Team features, plus advanced analytics, dedicated account management, and custom integrations.

Best For : Large organizations and enterprises with high-volume content needs .

5. Discounts and Trials :

- DeepSeek AI offers a 7-day free trial for the Pro and Team plans, allowing you to explore premium features before committing.

- Annual subscriptions come with a 20% discount compared to monthly billing.

Comparing DeepSeek AI with Other Tools

How does DeepSeek AI stack up against other content creation tools? Here's a comparative analysis:

DeepSeek AI vs. Grammarly

DeepSeek AI : Focuses on content generation, SEO optimization, and idea brainstorming. Ideal for end-to-end content creation.

Grammarly : Primarily a grammar and spell-checking tool. Best for editing and proofreading existing content.

2. DeepSeek AI vs. Jasper (formerly Jarvis)

DeepSeek AI : Offers a more affordable pricing structure with robust SEO and multilingual capabilities. Great for creators on a budget.

Jasper : Known for its advanced AI writing capabilities but comes at a higher price point. Best for users who prioritize creative writing.

3. DeepSeek AI vs. Surfer SEO

DeepSeek AI : Combines content creation with SEO optimization, making it a one-stop solution for creators.

Surfer SEO : Focuses exclusively on SEO analysis and optimization. Best for users who already have a content creation workflow in place.

4. DeepSeek AI vs. Copy.ai

DeepSeek AI : Offers a broader range of features, including plagiarism detection, multilingual support, and team collaboration tools.

Copy.ai : Specializes in short-form content like ad copy and social media posts. Best for marketers focused on specific content types.

5. Why Choose DeepSeek AI?

Versatility : DeepSeek AI supports a wide range of content formats, from blogs and social media posts to videos and e-commerce listings.

Affordability : Competitive pricing makes it accessible to creators of all levels.

Ease of Use : Intuitive interface and comprehensive support resources ensure a smooth user experience.

Innovation : Continuous updates and new features keep the platform at the forefront of AI-driven content creation.

Conclusion

DeepSeek AI is a versatile, user-friendly, and cost-effective tool that empowers content creators to streamline their workflows, enhance creativity, and achieve measurable results. By addressing common questions, providing troubleshooting support, and offering flexible pricing plans, DeepSeek AI ensures that creators of all levels can harness the power of AI to elevate their content. Whether you're comparing it to other tools or exploring its features for the first time, DeepSeek AI stands out as a reliable and innovative solution for modern content creation. Embrace the future of AI and unlock your full potential as a creator with DeepSeek AI.

Chapter 17: Embracing the Future of Content Creation

The Power of AI in Your Hands

DeepSeek AI empowers content creators to achieve new levels of creativity, efficiency, and success. Embrace the power of AI and transform your content creation process.

Transforming Your Creative Process

With DeepSeek AI, you can streamline your workflow, enhance your creativity, and produce content that resonates with your audience. Discover how AI can revolutionize your creative process.

Unlocking New Opportunities with DeepSeek AI

DeepSeek AI opens up new possibilities for content creators, from expanding your reach to exploring new formats and platforms. Unlock your full potential with the help of AI.

Chapter 18: Resources and Further Reading

DeepSeek AI Documentation and Tutorials

Access comprehensive documentation and tutorials to help you get the most out of DeepSeek AI.

Recommended Books and Articles

Explore a curated list of books and articles on AI, content creation, and digital marketing to deepen your knowledge and skills .

Online Communities and Forums

Join online communities and forums to connect with other content creators, share insights, and learn from industry experts.

Tools and Plugins to Complement DeepSeek AI

Discover additional tools and plugins that can enhance your content creation process and complement DeepSeek AI's capabilities.

Chapter 19: Glossary of Terms

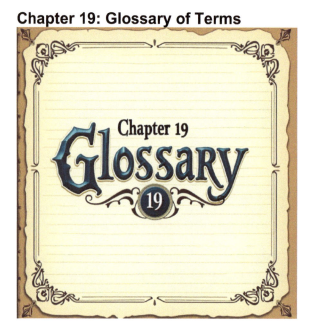

Artificial intelligence (AI) and content creation are fields rich with technical jargon and complex concepts. For creators looking to leverage tools like DeepSeek AI, understanding these terms is essential to maximizing their potential. This chapter provides a comprehensive glossary of key terms, simplifies technical jargon, and breaks down complex concepts into digestible explanations. Whether you're a beginner or an experienced user, this guide will help you navigate the world of AI-driven content creation with confidence.

Key AI and Content Creation Terminology

Here's a glossary of essential terms related to AI and content creation:

1. **Artificial Intelligence (AI) :** A branch of computer science focused on creating systems that can perform tasks typically requiring human intelligence, such as learning, reasoning, and problem-solving.

2. **Natural Language Processing (NLP) :** A subfield of AI that enables machines to understand, interpret, and generate human language. NLP powers tools like DeepSeek AI for tasks such as text generation and sentiment analysis.

3. **Machine Learning (ML) :** A subset of AI that involves training algorithms to learn patterns from data and make predictions or decisions without explicit programming.

4. **Generative AI :** AI systems capable of creating new content, such as text, images, or music, based on input data. Examples include GPT models and DALL·E.

5. **SEO (Search Engine Optimization) :** The practice of optimizing content to rank higher in search engine results, increasing visibility and organic traffic.

6. **Plagiarism :** The act of using someone else's work or ideas without proper attribution. AI tools like DeepSeek AI include plagiarism detection to ensure content originality.

7. **Content Automation :** The use of technology, such as AI, to automate repetitive content creation tasks, such as writing, editing, and publishing.

8. **Tone and Style :** The voice and manner in which content is written. AI tools can adapt tone and style to match brand guidelines or audience preferences.

9. **Multilingual Support :** The ability of a tool to understand, generate, and translate content in multiple languages.

10. **Algorithm :** A set of rules or instructions that an AI system follows to perform tasks or solve problems.

11. **Data Training :** The process of feeding data into an AI system to help it learn and improve its performance over time.

12. Chatbot : An AI-powered program designed to simulate conversation with users, often used for customer service or engagement.

13. Sentiment Analysis : An NLP technique used to determine the emotional tone behind a piece of text, such as positive, negative, or neutral.

14. Content Personalization : Tailoring content to individual users based on their preferences, behaviors, or demographics.

15. Metadata : Data that provides information about other data, such as titles, descriptions, and tags used to optimize content for search engines.

16. A/B Testing : A method of comparing two versions of content to determine which performs better in terms of engagement or conversions.

17. Deep Learning : A subset of machine learning that uses neural networks to model complex patterns in data, often used for tasks like image and speech recognition.

18. API (Application Programming Interface) : A set of protocols that allows different software applications to communicate with each other. DeepSeek AI offers APIs for seamless integration with other tools.

19. Content Localization : Adapting content to suit the cultural, linguistic, and regional preferences of a specific audience.

20. Ethical AI : The practice of developing and using AI systems in a way that is transparent, fair, and accountable.

Understanding Technical Jargon

AI and content creation can feel overwhelming due to the abundance of technical terms. Here's a simplified breakdown of some commonly used jargon:

1. Neural Networks : Inspired by the human brain, neural networks are a series of algorithms that recognize patterns in data. They are the foundation of many AI systems.

2. Training Data : The dataset used to teach an AI model how to perform a specific task. For example, DeepSeek AI uses vast amounts of text data to learn how to generate human-like content.

3. Tokenization : The process of breaking down text into smaller units, such as words or phrases, to help AI systems analyze and process language.

4. Transformer Models : A type of neural network architecture used in NLP tasks. GPT (Generative Pre-trained

Transformer) models, like those used by DeepSeek AI, are examples of transformer models.

5. **Latent Space** : A representation of data in a simplified form that AI systems use to identify patterns and relationships.

6. **Overfitting** : When an AI model performs well on training data but poorly on new, unseen data. This is a common challenge in machine learning.

7. **Bias in AI** : The tendency of AI systems to produce skewed or unfair results due to biased training data or algorithms. Ethical AI practices aim to minimize bias.

8. **Zero-Shot Learning** : The ability of an AI model to perform tasks it hasn't explicitly been trained on, using its general understanding of language.

9. **Fine-Tuning** : The process of adapting a pre-trained AI model to perform a specific task more effectively.

10. **Reinforcement Learning** :
A type of machine learning where an AI system learns by receiving feedback in the form of rewards or penalties.

Simplifying Complex Concepts
To help you better understand how DeepSeek AI works and how it can benefit you, here's a simplified explanation of some complex AI concepts:
1. How AI Generates Content :

- DeepSeek AI uses NLP and machine learning to analyze patterns in text data. When you input a prompt, the AI predicts the most likely sequence of words to generate coherent and contextually relevant content.

- **Example:** If you ask DeepSeek AI to write a blog post about "healthy eating," it uses its training data to generate a well-structured article with relevant information.

2. How SEO Optimization Works :

- DeepSeek AI analyzes your content and suggests improvements to make it more search-engine-friendly. This includes optimizing keywords, meta descriptions, and headings.

- **Example:** If you're writing a product description, DeepSeek AI might suggest adding high-ranking keywords like "affordable" or "eco-friendly" to improve visibility.

3. How Plagiarism Detection Works :

- DeepSeek AI compares your content against a vast database of existing texts to identify similarities. If it detects potential plagiarism, it highlights the sections and suggests revisions.

- **Example:** If you accidentally use a phrase that appears in another article, DeepSeek AI will flag it and recommend rephrasing.

4. How Multilingual Support Works :

- DeepSeek AI uses NLP models trained on multiple languages to understand and generate content in different languages. It also considers cultural nuances to ensure translations are accurate and relevant.

Example: If you're targeting a Spanish-speaking audience, DeepSeek AI can translate your English content into Spanish while maintaining the original tone and style.

5. How Personalization Works :

- DeepSeek AI analyzes user data, such as browsing history and preferences, to tailor content to individual needs. This ensures your content resonates with your target audience.

Example: If you're running an email campaign, DeepSeek AI can personalize subject lines and content based on each recipient's interests.

Solutions to Common Challenges

Understanding AI and content creation terminology can be challenging. Here are some solutions to common issues:

1. Challenge: Overwhelmed by Technical Terms

Solution : Use this glossary as a reference guide. Bookmark it and revisit it whenever you encounter unfamiliar terms.

2. Challenge: Misunderstanding AI Capabilities

Solution : Focus on practical applications. For example, instead of worrying about how neural networks work, explore how DeepSeek AI can help you write better blog posts.

3. Challenge: Applying AI Concepts to Real-World Scenarios

Solution : Start small. Use DeepSeek AI for simple tasks like generating social media captions, and gradually explore more advanced features as you become comfortable.

4. Challenge: Keeping Up with Evolving Terminology

Solution : Stay informed by following AI blogs, attending webinars, and participating in online communities. DeepSeek AI's Help Center also provides updates on new features and terminology.

Conclusion

Understanding the terminology and concepts behind AI and content creation is key to unlocking the full potential of tools like DeepSeek AI. This glossary simplifies complex ideas, making them accessible to creators of all levels. By demystifying technical jargon and providing practical solutions, DeepSeek AI ensures that you can confidently navigate the world of AI-driven content creation. Embrace the power of AI and take your content to new heights with DeepSeek AI.

Chapter 20: About DeepSeek AI

DeepSeek AI is more than just a platform—it's a movement to revolutionize content creation through the power of artificial intelligence. This chapter delves into the company's origins, mission, and vision, highlighting its commitment to innovation, excellence, and customer support. Whether you're a new user or a long-time advocate, this chapter provides a comprehensive look at the people and principles behind DeepSeek AI.

The Company Behind the Technology

DeepSeek AI was founded by a team of AI enthusiasts, engineers, and content creators who recognized the challenges faced by modern creators. With the rapid growth of digital content, the demand for high-quality, engaging, and consistent material has never been higher. DeepSeek AI was born out of a desire to empower creators with tools that streamline workflows, enhance creativity, and deliver measurable results.

Founding Principles :

Empowerment : DeepSeek AI believes in empowering creators of all levels, from beginners to seasoned professionals, with accessible and intuitive AI tools.

Innovation : The company is committed to staying at the forefront of AI technology, continuously improving its platform to meet the evolving needs of creators.

Collaboration : DeepSeek AI views itself as a partner in the creative process, working alongside creators to bring their visions to life.

Core Values :

User-Centric Design : Every feature and update is designed with the user in mind, ensuring a seamless and enjoyable experience.

Transparency : DeepSeek AI prioritizes ethical AI practices, ensuring transparency in how its tools are developed and used.

Community Engagement : The company actively engages with its user base, gathering feedback and fostering a sense of community among creators.

Mission and Vision

DeepSeek AI is driven by a clear mission and a bold vision for the future of content creation.

Mission :

DeepSeek AI's mission is to empower content creators with cutting-edge AI tools that enhance creativity, streamline workflows, and deliver exceptional results. By democratizing access to advanced technology, the company aims to level the playing field for creators worldwide.

Vision :

DeepSeek AI envisions a future where AI and human creativity work hand in hand to produce content that inspires, informs, and entertains. The company strives to be a global leader in AI-driven content creation, setting new standards for innovation, quality, and ethical practices.

Goals :

Expand Accessibility : Make AI tools accessible to creators of all backgrounds and skill levels.

Foster Innovation : Continuously push the boundaries of what AI can achieve in content creation.

Build Community : Create a global network of creators who share knowledge, collaborate, and grow together.

Commitment to Innovation and Excellence

DeepSeek AI is dedicated to delivering high-quality solutions that meet the needs of content creators worldwide. This commitment is reflected in every aspect of the company's operations, from product development to customer support.

Innovation in Action :

Advanced NLP Models : DeepSeek AI leverages state-of-the-art Natural Language Processing (NLP) models to provide accurate, context-aware content generation.

Continuous Updates : The platform is regularly updated with new features, tools, and improvements based on user feedback and technological advancements.

Research and Development : DeepSeek AI invests heavily in R&D to explore new applications of AI in content creation, such as visual and audio content generation.

Excellence in Delivery :

User-Friendly Interface : DeepSeek AI's intuitive design ensures that even beginners can navigate the platform with ease.

High-Quality Output : The platform's algorithms are trained on vast datasets to ensure that generated content is accurate, relevant, and engaging.

Ethical Practices : DeepSeek AI adheres to strict ethical guidelines, ensuring that its tools are used responsibly and transparently.

Customer-Centric Approach :

Feedback-Driven Development : User feedback is at the heart of DeepSeek AI's development process. The company actively seeks input from its community to shape future updates and features.

Educational Resources : DeepSeek AI provides a wealth of tutorials, guides, and webinars to help users maximize the platform's potential.

Dedicated Support : The company offers robust customer support to address any issues or questions users may have.

Contact Information and Support

DeepSeek AI is committed to providing exceptional support to its users. Whether you need technical assistance, have questions about pricing, or want to share feedback, the company offers multiple channels for communication.

Support Options :

1. **Help Center :**

   - Access a comprehensive library of tutorials, FAQs, and troubleshooting guides.

   - Visit:

https://deepseekai.com/help

2. **Live Chat:**

   - Get instant assistance from DeepSeek AI's support team via live chat on the website.

   - Available: Monday–Friday, 9 AM–6 PM (GMT)

3. **Email Support :**

   - Send your queries to support@deepseekai.com for a detailed response within 24 hours.

4. Community Forum:

- Join DeepSeek AI's online community to connect with other users, share tips, and discuss best practices.

- Visit:

https://deepseekai.com/community

5. Social Media:

- Follow DeepSeek AI on social media for updates, tips, and announcements:

- Twitter: [@DeepSeekAI](https://twitter.com/DeepSeekAI)

- LinkedIn: [DeepSeek AI](https://linkedin.com/company/deepseekai)

- Instagram:

[@DeepSeekAI](https://instagram.com/DeepSeekAI)

6. Enterprise Support:

- For enterprise clients, DeepSeek AI offers dedicated account managers and priority support. Contact enterprise@deepseekai.com for more information.

Conclusion

DeepSeek AI is more than just a technology company—it's a partner in your creative journey. With a mission to empower creators, a vision for the future of content creation, and a commitment to innovation and excellence, DeepSeek AI is redefining what's possible in the digital age. Whether you're a blogger, marketer, video creator, or e-commerce brand, DeepSeek AI provides the tools and support you need to succeed. Explore the platform, connect with the community, and discover how DeepSeek AI can transform your content creation process. The future of creativity is here, and it starts with DeepSeek AI.

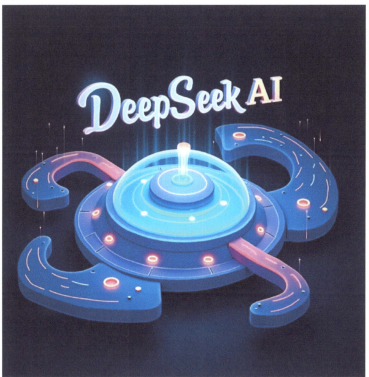

Final Thoughts

DeepSeek AI is more than just a tool—it's a game-changer for content creators. By leveraging the power of AI, you can enhance your creativity, streamline your workflow, and achieve new levels of success. Whether you're a blogger, social media influencer, video creator, or marketer, DeepSeek AI has something to offer. Embrace the future of content creation and unlock your full potential with DeepSeek AI.

---

www.ingramcontent.com/pod-product-compliance
Lightning Source LLC
LaVergne TN
LVHW072049060326
832903LV00053B/312